I0813234

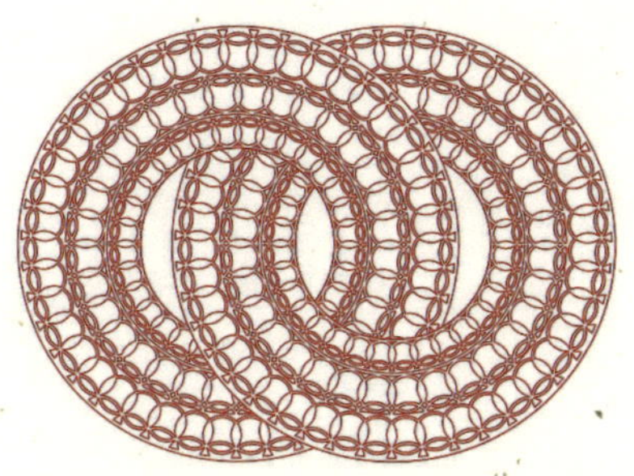

THE JERSEY SLIDE

THE JERSEY SLIDE

DANNY SHOT

CAVANKERRY
PRESS

CavanKerry Press Ltd.
Fort Lee, New Jersey
www.cavankerrypress.org

Publisher's Cataloging-in-Publication Data
provided by Five Rainbows Cataloging Services

Names: Shot, Danny, author.
Title: The Jersey slide / Danny Shot.
Description: Fort Lee, NJ : CavanKerry Press, 2025.
Identifiers: ISBN 978-1-960327-14-7 (paperback)
Subjects: LCSH: Families--Poetry. | Baseball--Poetry. | Emigration and immigration--Poetry. | American poetry--21st century. | Jewish poetry. | Beat poetry, American. | BISAC: POETRY / Jewish. | POETRY / Subjects & Themes / Family. | POETRY / American / General.
Classification: LCC PS3619.H68 J47 2025 (print) | DDC 811/.6--dc23.

Cover artwork: Robert Piersanti
Author photo: John Dalton

Cover and interior text design by Mike Corrao
First Edition 2025, Printed in the United States of America

Florenz Eisman Memorial Series

CavanKerry Press is proud to present the seventh book in the Florenz Eisman Memorial Series—fine collections by New Jersey poets, notable or emerging. A gifted poet and great lover of poetry herself, Florenz was the publisher partner in establishing the press and CavanKerry Managing Editor from its inception in 2000 until her passing in 2013. Her ideas and intelligence were a great source of inspiration for writers and staff alike as were her quick wit and signature red lipstick.

Made possible by funds from the New Jersey State Council on the Arts, a partner agency of the National Endowment for the Arts.

NATIONAL ENDOWMENT for the ARTS
arts.gov

CavanKerry Press is grateful for the generous support it has received from the New Jersey State Council on the Arts, as well as the following funders:

The Academy of American Poets
Bergen County Arts
Community of Literary Magazines and Presses
National Book Foundation
New Jersey Arts and Culture Renewal Fund
New Jersey Council for the Humanities
New Jersey Cultural Trust
New Jersey Economic Development Authority
The Poetry Foundation

ALSO BY DANNY SHOT

Night Bird Flying (2025)
WORKS (2018)

Well I'll keep on moving, moving on
Things are bound to be improving these days . . .

"These Days" by Jackson Browne (written at 16 years of age),
sung by Nico on *Chelsea Girl* in 1967,
channeled by Tammy Faye Starlite in 2023

CONTENTS

I.

Tempest

All the poets who ever writ
are here with me
I raise the mainsail up the mast
for those who've passed into the night alive within us
the closeted friend too ashamed to seek treatment until too late
a black-hatted Nuyorican legend lugging a condom crucifix
singing songs of Puerto Rican liberation
the blind professor holding court
upon a smoky couch welcoming all who sail
through open door to introduce themselves.

I stand before you
bent but unbowed
gray but not dead
anonymous and proud.

Some poets have tied their sails and souls
to the warm comforts of the academy
rare few have cast off against the prevailing gales
emerging as prophet for their motley crew of misfits
others became unmoored by the cruel vicissitudes of fashion
unable or unwilling to follow the wind
a few have fallen into the doldrums, pounding out despaired
manifestoes to the sound of Mahler on broke down radios in
half lit rooms.
Hyacinths for the disappeared thrown into the roiling sea
so-called enemies of state, victims of the dictator's purge
and those destroyed by madness and lack of recognition.

Yet here I stand
creased by absurd laughter
unembittered by rejection

breathless in love with the elusive
beauty of words spoken into the void.

To all the poets who ever lived
proclaiming God's glory in the Judean desert
telling tales of epic wanderings off Ionian shores
griots singing praise-songs calling on ancestors' protection
besotted flaneurs absinthe blind scribbling in tattered notebooks
the muscle bound hod carrier from way out west who broke
his back under the weight of belief that poetry could save our souls
the feminist icon brooding at her kitchen table over her terminal
    diagnosis
a candy store owner holding intricate jazz lines
in his head while serving soda pop to thirsty teens
the working-class Brooklyn Jew who found his distinctive
voice later in life and couldn't stop sharing
a singular woman writing shapeless verse
to no one and everyone simultaneously.

I call you forth
here upon this rugged deck
enveloped in the foggy soup
between wreckage and time
memory and consciousness.

Sail with us upon the choppy waves.

The Meaning of Life

Willie Mays Topps 1966
baseball card in my hand,
final season batting average: .317
homeruns for 1965: 52,
the most majestic
number on the card
#1, first in the series.

My first baseball game
Yankee Stadium, 1967.
My father and Leo
and Mickey Mantle's
500th home run.
Back then 500 home runs
was impressive.

I was born a few blocks
from Yankee Stadium.
We were never Yankee fans.
I'll chalk it up to the fact
that we're Jews.

My dad, a Giants man
switched allegiance in 1962
when a new National League
team made its debut.
Brooklyn Dodger fans never got over it.
Giants fans accepted betrayal.
We were Mets fans, but
Willie Mays our baseball god.

My father was long gone
when I worked at Macy's
selling china on the 8th floor,

right next to Santa Land.
I met Caroline there.
She sold crystal.
Men (not much more than boys)
sold china, women sold crystal.

One day Willie Mays and
another man walked in
for a set of china.
After half an hour
he decided on
Franciscan Desert Rose
service for eight and
all the various serving pieces.
Honestly — that would not
have been my choice.
No accounting for taste.
I still have a carbon copy
of the sales receipt
with his signature.

My favorite city is San Francisco.
I've been there six times.
I lived there for a year with my girlfriend.
After I left her
she came back home and died
of a drug overdose.
I'm a diehard Mets fan, but
my second favorite team
is the San Francisco Giants.
Willie's Giants.

In 1969 we took Mom
to Shea Stadium for Mother's Day.
Tom Seaver beat Juan Marichal
one to nothing

one of the best pitched games
in history. During that game
my mom read *The Godfather*
cover to cover
grateful for the opportunity
to read undisturbed
among 50,000 screaming fans.
Juan Marichal pitched 13 innings
and allowed only 5 hits
and he lost.
Tom Seaver died last year
same time as my sister.

I miss San Francisco.
A recurring dream:
I'm trying to find City Lights
but the roads have changed
and I can't find my way.
Maps show me how to find
the ocean, or Coit Tower,
or Golden Gate Park,
but not my favorite bookstore.

As long as Willie Mays is alive,
fucked up as our country is,
it's not as fucked as it can be.
Enough about family damage.
A world with Willie Mays —
still a world worth living in.

Postscript: Willie Mays passed away June 18, 2024.
Still, we move forward.

Hero Worship

Patti's heroes are my heroes:
Rimbaud, Ginsberg, Dylan,
Burroughs, Corso, Houdini,
Joan of Arc, Marianne Faithful.
I must have found a few on my own.
Patti Smith is my hero.

I met her once, up close
like this close
at St. Mark's Poetry Project.
It was awkward.
I tried to give her a book of poems
by Jack Wiler — *I Have No Clue*.
Jack from Wenonah,
small town South Jersey,
Patti from Vineland
or thereabouts,
Jack 5 years older than me,
5 younger than Patti,
(the first time I met Jack
he said, "I thought you
and Eliot Katz were old guys,
Jesus Christ, you're just a kid."
I was 22)
so I thought she might like the book.

Anxious, I took a step
towards Patti
handing the book to her.
She took a step back.

"This is a book," I said. "I got a book for you."
She took a step back.
"A book. For you. I got a book."

Another step back.
"This is for you. A book."
Allen Ginsberg, close by
came over
put his arm around me —
"This is my friend Danny,
he wants to give you a book" —
and guided my hands forward to Patti
who reached out,
nervous smile on her face
to take the book.
"Thanks," she said
disappearing.

Today I'm reading *M Train*,
A book friends have warned me about,
"It's not *Just Kids* you know."
Maybe that's why I like it better
as I discover new heroes.
Thank you Patti Smith
spirit guide, hero.

Kids

He is my favorite photographer.
"I've been taking pictures of skateboarders,"
he said, "They're fantastic."
We made arrangements for me to come to his loft
in Tribeca and pick out some photos.

When I got to his door, a young voice told me
he was across the street at the Baby Doll Lounge.
He was sitting at the bar staring straight up
a stripper's crotch. I tapped him on the shoulder,
"I'm here for some photos." He was confused,
"Here? I don't think they want us to take photos."
"No," I said, "of skateboarders for my magazine."
"Oh," he said, "of course. Have a seat. What're you drinking?"
"Beer," I replied.
"You're a poet, right? Poets drink whiskey. I'm buying."

Five or six drinks later his easy banter
with the working girls was getting
more worrying with each completed drink.
"My friend here's a poet. Poets eat pussy,
what've you got for him?"
A bouncer who had been standing by the door
grabbed him in a bearhug and deposited him
on the sidewalk outside. I wanted to protest
but meekly followed.

We walked across the street to his loft.
Inside was a group of eight or nine
teenagers lounging around,
skateboards parked near the door.

Four or five of them, mostly girls,
crumpled in a heap
on a futon by the wall.
Four others were playing darts
on the other side of the room.
Instead of hitting the target,
the object of the game was to catch
the dart before it hit the board.
The famous photographer walked to the counter
and opened a fresh bottle of whiskey,
pouring full glasses
for me and him before retiring
to a chair in front of the coffee table.

A few packets of photos lay on the table.

The teens were in various states of injury.
One kid had a dart stuck in his arm;
others were bleeding from various wounds.
The famous photographer looked over the carnage —
"Kids, what're you gonna do?" — and passed out.

I played Florence Nightingale,
finding rubbing alcohol, cotton balls and Band-Aids
in the medicine cabinet. The teens were compliant,
friendly, and not the least bit curious
about what was going on.
After maybe half an hour
the famous photographer
opened his eyes —
"Kids, aren't they fantastic?
I should make a movie."

In a Bottle

Red yellow white black pink dabs
speckle drunken bottles of Cutty Sark
Seagrams Bacardi Martini and Rossi
which he gave as gifts. We have 4 art bottles.
Of course, Hersch did more than paint bottles,
a beat jazz poet, the real thing
pen pal of Ginsberg and Corso,
owner of Hersch's Beehive candy store
home base for generations of Bayonne youth
immortalized in the children's book *Hep Cat*
a Navy vet of WWII and Korea
a family man in love with do it yourself
creations, in love with his Corona typewriter,
copy machine and laminator.

Hersch was a real mensch.
Maybe the last of his kind.
My teen sons played a ragged version of *Children*
of the Grave at the Bowery Poetry Club
for a Father's Day celebration of Hersch
during his 85th year. At the nursing home
Perry Robinson, Gerry Drums, Bob Holman
and I serenaded him the day before his death.

Last week, Caroline and I dog sat
for Levi's dog Uli, whose favorite game
is catch the rat, fun for the first day or so
but worn thin as she tried to claw her way
under the stereo, nails scratching floor
in frantic attempts to catch the imaginary rat.
Caroline blocked the space with a portable safe,

an old IBM Selectric, a painted Cutty Sark bottle
filled with water to give it some heft.
After a day or two Uli forgot the game.

When Uli left we dismantled the barricade.
As Caroline emptied the bottle,
a dollar fell out, then another, and another
and so on. Hallelujah! The bottle was filled
with money. Herschel Silverman
your memory is a blessing!

(Hopper's) Muse

Outside. Through the window. Get my ass up and out. I spend my days like this. How many days? The sweats stopped. I'm not shaking today. I can't apologize for what's already broken.

Maybe it's me. The waves, the crashing waves . . . The sea has passed. The mess cleaned up. Somehow. I wonder where he is. Did he drive away? Drive him away? Me. . . I don't blame.

I was awful. I am awful. He left me. I deserved it. Unlovable me. Then he came back. Damn him. This city supposed to be a fresh start. Philly was too small. Simply too Philly.

Ready to take this city by storm. Chestnuts in Central Park. Midnight at The Ritz. *Guys and Dolls*. Who ever conquered New York? There's a story here somewhere but it's lost in a cloud.

I'm an artist too. He doesn't believe me. Or he believes me and doesn't care. Lonely lonely muse. Unlovable vessel. I like to paint pictures. I'm as good as he is. I, I, I, I sound crazy.

I like my drugs too. He's out there hustling pictures to the hoity-toity art fuckers. I'm frozen staring out the window at the warehouse roofs wondering when my time. . . when I get clean.

The sky is blue and I can't move. Paralyzed he's gone for good. Off this bed, out this coffin. No dope, no crutch, no self-inflicted wounds. Hope he's gone for good.

Jesus is a bad metaphor. I don't need salvation. Across the horizon, a place to start anew. New Jersey? Suspicious. I need, I need, I need . . . This can be my city too. New York is my oyster —

Whatever that means. I can paint. I know my way around a color wheel. Wavelength, relationships, odd combinations. All I got to do is slip on my shoes and walk out that door.

He should be coming back soon. I can wait. Maybe he's scored. Close my eyes, let the dream take hold. Sailing, floating over waves that crash land on my unrequited soul.

I can't wait. Flying over the roofs of Manhattan like Chagall's lovers, like Peter Pan drifting through skyscraper haze. Comfortable, self-possessed, lighter than air. If only . . . if only . . .

I can get off this bed, put on my overcoat. Into a new life. Free of necessity. Free of this curse that's really my savior. The city a mirage to melt into if only I move. I think I can.

Out the door. Down the steps. Out of the picture. Into my own life. The star of my very own film. A shit reality show. Maybe. I'm not a picture. A picture maker. He has to know that.

Why does he keep me? Hope he brings back a treat. Stop looking through the glass, damn it! Bridge splash. Through my window. Crisis of confidence. Terminal crisis. Confidence man.

He's not keeping me here. I'm doing this to myself. Icarus wings. There is a way out. The other side of this deception. The beckoning stars. Sirius. The window. I can fly . . .

NY Story

— for Jeff Wright

Sorry I missed your reading
I didn't know about it
I was down the shore
Had to wash my hair
The Jets were in the playoffs
The in-laws were in town
Vicious hangover
Been feeling insubstantial
The train got stuck underground
A passenger was sick
Someone fell on the tracks
I thought it was next week
The kids showed up unannounced
The evening news was deflating
She wouldn't stop talking
Too many glasses of wine
Found a spot on my forehead
My ex bummed me out
Had a serious migraine
The internet went down
I was coughing and worried
what people might say
The keys couldn't be found

I didn't want to run into Manny
Didi said you canceled
I was watching *Mrs. Maisel*
and lost track of time
The fridge lost power
Sorry bro, I just forgot

Hurt my ankle on the treadmill
The weather said torrential rain
Bootsy coughed up a hairball
The sushi buffet was a mistake
I was stuck on the couch
The weed was too strong
Got scared to go out
Was caught in a maelstrom
Lost an earring in the shower
Can I watch it on YouTube?
When are you doing it again?
Maybe next week
I'll do my best to come
Trust me, I'll be there

Presentation of Self as Performance Piece

you see yourself as a bon vivant
a distinguished man of letters
in reality you are a retired English teacher
still trying to find his place in the world

Does it matter you once were a Punk?

others see you as popular
and somewhat successful
you work real hard not to be
forgotten on a daily basis

And before that a hippie?

you tell it like it is
free of artifice
well, you don't lie
but sometimes have a tough time
distinguishing fantasy from reality

More committed to pussy than philosophy

you impress your family
with your *Jeopardy* prowess
have concerns about
dimming memory

Remember what Kant told you long ago:

you are a good friend
a good listener
a good father
wondering if you have made
a difference at all

Stick to the truth, it's easy to remember

you think you have myriad identities
husband, father, teacher, poet
the world sees you as Jew
an old one at that

Hmmm, or was it Twain?

you fancy yourself a Whitmanic bard
lately you have more in common with Emily Dickinson

I am large, I contain multitudes . . .
I'm nobody! Who are you?

Open Mic at Shades of Green

I'm too old for this place.
I order another drink anyway.
Tired of the poets, I sit at the bar
talking to the Irish tourist
who's 40 years younger
and mad at her husband
for reasons I can't comprehend.

Just then Dave brings me a drink
he got from the other bartender
by mistake. The Irish tourist
likes me even better.
"He's not my boyfriend," I explain,
but she doesn't believe me
and invites me back to the hotel.

"No thanks," I say. "I'm here for the poetry."
"That's too bad," she says. I agree.
"Do you know Patrick Kavanaugh?"
she asks. "Can't say I've met him,
but there was a night a few years
ago, when high on mescaline
with 2 younger coworkers we
listened to a recording and laughed
our heads off. Almost literally."

My name is called.
I walk to the stage.
Read a poem about
my sister's suffering.

A smattering of applause.
The tourist is gone.
Long walk across Manhattan.
Train to New Jersey.
Dreams of immortality.

Art

Sometimes you try too hard.
You hate yourself for that.
You are polite to people
who have no use for you.
You rush your family and friends
to be early for things
that start too late.
You say too much
forever telling your story
instead of seeking that place
where art and words meet
beyond narrative,
that inexplicable spot.

The feel of the life force
the spontaneous kiss
the guitar thrum
Chagall's flying lovers
the oak tree on the corner
the life that speaks
a different language
or no language at all
that you know is real
and alive.

II.

The Jersey Slide

Birds of Bayonne

Follow the path in Bayonne,
snowy egrets
fish for whatever
they can dredge up cawing
to the Turnpike overpass
cars crawl, honk, clamor,
Jersey Slide, crisscross,
cook the asphalt skyway.

Colossus

We gaze at your backside — what a glorious ass it is,
mother of exiles. We're the ones who heed your call,
striving across the river, the racing heart of Manhattan,
beacon of liberty and wealth and perhaps the making it,
whatever that means, whatever that meant.

You called me

a replacement child and I had to laugh
because I never thought of it that way.
One life can't replace another as Ronnie
James Dio couldn't replace Ozzy or Trump
can't replace Obama. If anyone's
a replacement child it's Carol, not me.

Fuck You

you fucking fuck. Carlos sits sullenly
in the back of the class in his inside out
tee shirt wondering when it was that you
became such a dick.

Age

A middle-aged woman wearing a Dumont
hoodie walks toward me by the river.
"Hey," I shout, "I'm from Dumont." She looks
at me, perhaps frightened, her Dumbledore
sweatshirt glittering in the fog.

Overheard by the Urinals

. . . and I told him twice
Never bring a dog around
an open casket.

Revelation

Unfortunately, my wife came
to the conclusion that I was
old before I did, and now
anything I do proves it so.

Two Jews in a small town

on Christmas Day. We meet at 7-11, smoke
some weed, share a Slurpee, don't know what
to do. Sheila says Grateful Dead, you say Sabbath.
She walks alone in the snow. You stand frozen.

Winefest JC

All pretense of tasting wine
forgotten as we move
from line to line,
plastic cups in hand.
The murky
field lit by klieg lights

casting improbable shadows
on the soggy soil.
Caroline and I take selfie
after selfie, the illusion
of dangling shadow penises
which we find
uproarious and send
to friends and our kids
who are not amused.

After the Deluge, Part 21

We join the neighbors in the street
at 1 a.m., glasses of whiskey in hand
soaking wet, sore from bailing
the torrents rushing into our basement.

These once in a lifetime weather events
have become a way of life around here.
We clink our glasses in the rain.
To a better tomorrow! A better tomorrow?

Why I'm a Mets Fan

Because the Dodgers signed Jackie Robinson in 1947
Because Willie Mays played for the NY Giants
Because the Yankees waited until 1955 to play Elston Howard
Because Tom Seaver
Because I believe in miracles
Because I'm a Jew
Because of my dad
Because I love a good cry
Because Jacob de Grom is pitching today
Because baseball is what's best about America
Because none of this will make sense to a Yankees fan

Inevitable

Do you know Irv Feldman? asks

the homeless man in front of 7-11.

No, I reply, why do you ask?

He died.

I'm sorry, I reply.

He was an old Jewish man, a good guy.

Sorry to hear that, I say.

You remind me of him.

Sorry to hear that . . .

A Sunday in March

I'm sitting in a church hall in JC
with a whole bunch of Ukrainian
and Afghan refugees,
kids running all over the place.
People seem genuinely happy
to be able to speak to each other
in their native languages.

When I picked my designated family up,
Yulia the mother seemed taciturn
and maybe sad. Now she is laughing
with the other women.
We're supposed to leave at 2:30
but I don't want to drag her away.

The women are now exchanging numbers
and a few of them are crying
which makes me want to cry
though of course I won't.

This must be how my mother once felt.
Maybe.

II.

I'll tell you how it ended
which might make you laugh.
It made me laugh. Another family
who Yulia met asked if I could give
them a ride home as they lived
a few towns from Yulia.
I said, "Sure."

The man said, "How much?"
They all thought I was an Uber driver.
On the way back the women were laughing
and talking nonstop. I dropped Yulia
and her son off in Hackensack.
The man spoke a little English,
his wife and son, none at all.
I had explained that I was doing this
as volunteer work for the Hoboken Synagogue
(where I am not a member, but a friend of the Rabbi).
As I let them out by their home he said, "How much?"
I told him the ride was free.
He said, "You said you were Jewish?"
I laughed.
His wife heard us laughing.
I think she asked what we were laughing at.
He said something but I heard the word *Juden*.
She reached into her pocketbook
and started pulling out money.
I was like *no, no, no,* all smiles.
As they left my car, he came over
to my side to hug me.
"You a rare, remarkable man,"
he said before leaving.

Wreckage

I am trying to figure this out.
I don't have the answer.
What I know:
Our country has gone crazy —
Today is uncomfortable for most everyone.
We can't not talk about racism any longer
We need to hear each other's pain.

What I hear:
Sirens, weeks and months of sirens —
the totemic sound of America today
helicopters flying low overhead
chants resounding through the steel
and granite canyons.
Say the name: Fill in the blank
The pop! pop! pop! of flash grenades
the close-range bang! of rubber bullets
tear gas snaking through city streets
wooden batons cracking against bones
I hear America breaking piece by piece.

What I see (mostly on TV):
Macy's Herald Square on fire
ominous graffiti of rage
The Grand Concourse in shards
of glass and looted merchandise
Fort Greene a daily tinderbox.

Smell the brimstone in the air.
I am so tired of all this winning.

Last Night at Maxwell's

Jim D's funeral was not here
but in Long Island, where he grew up.
His memorial is here, and so are we.
Three generations of Hoboken hipsters
gathered in honor of Jim D
and the glory of rock and roll.

We send him off in style, Jersey style.
On stage his bass and cowboy hat
and band after band after band . . .
louder faster more and more . . .

A community that once was
spilling onto the sidewalk
smoking post-mortem cigarettes
oblivious to morning's call to work
together for one more night
in a place we still call home.

Debra

We play DJ with each other
and oh yeah we drank
tequila it was glorious
Everybody Rules the World
Velvet Underground
and *Sweet Melissa*

We walk arm in arm
down 6th Avenue
nothing has ever been
better They are looking
at us We are beautiful
We own the street
We own the night

Before Lunch

Am I the only person in New York
who looks at people's tee shirts?
I read them and comment,
often to the chagrin of the harried New Yorker
who invariably becomes dumbstruck
and quickens their pace away from
this perhaps creepy old man
who fancies himself a keen observer
of the human condition.
My wife is often embarrassed by my penchant
for starting conversations with strangers
over apparent trivialities.

I'm disappointed when people don't notice my t-shirt.

I walk through this museum filled with Tiffany lamps
and silver serving platters, not fertile grounds
for the words I want to write today, out across
the street to Central Park to the cavalcade
of messages sauntering and jogging by.
It's the 4th of May, I'm just a visitor.

The city glides past, as I remain stationary
in my spot beneath a sad willow.
Car horns tourists jabbering dim background
to the parade of wearable words and images passing by —
Will Work For Coffee . . . Jack Daniels . . . Harvard . . . Star Wars . . .
Wakanda . . . TD Bank Corporate Challenge . . . San Francisco 49ers . . .
Adidas . . . I Drink and I Know Things . . . Imagine . . .

Yoko Ono's Grapefruit . . . Run Baby Run . . . Point Reyes . . .
New Jersey — Only the Strong Survive . . . Notorious RBG . . .
Bank of America . . . Revolution . . . LL Bean . . . Obey . . . Louis Vuitton . . .
flock of crows on a bare tree branch . . . NYC . . . NYC . . . NYC . . .

Back to Tiffany's. My leg has fallen asleep. Time for lunch.

For Eva

What you call kindness
is sometimes me stating the obvious.
You are late, I wait, glad
to be with you on a day like this.

More than a nothing day really,
I try to match wits to no avail
slow tongued and plodding,
my entire life swirls around.

I wish it would stop
not my life but the swirl.
The dead won't leave me alone.

Driving over the 7th circle of hell
namely the Pulaski Skyway built obsolete
before complete, Southside Johnny warbling
on the radio "I Don't Want to Go Home"

as you offer running commentary
on the driving habits of New Jersey.
A silver Mercedes zigzags across lanes —
the Jersey Slide.

I am prone to pronouncements
You make small observations
riddled with allegory
General Pulaski was a so-and-so . . .

I overshare the past. Again.
You call me a replacement child,

but I'm the happy idiot of my family,
the one born into, the one I raised.

My mom called me good-time Charlie . . .
You ask questions I don't understand.
I smile, I nod, I smile some more.

Let's enjoy the September sun.
This isn't history class, let's call it life,
the shifting earth beneath our feet.

We trek past silk factory ruins
along the chromium banks of the Passaic —
The Great Falls of Paterson . . .

Then the slabby cemetery
below ominous power lines
idling refrigerator trucks hummmm . . .
under the bluest skies Jersey can offer

a little slice of heaven in Newark
sunflowers in hand
looking for Ginsberg's grave.

We sit outside generic Hoboken bar drinking
sad Red Needles, tequila and cranberry,
in honor of Leonard Cohen on his birthday

discussing endangered writers like
Philip Roth or Mordechai Richler
(A moot point since both are dead)

on what I planned to
be a literary day which has

taken a turn towards the Jewy,
as it so often does.

These are my happy places
shared with a new friend.
Looking home through your eyes
makes it new, meaning infused.

Old friends bring up memories
I wish they wouldn't, the nicknames,
the shit I made up but don't remember,
the inevitable surrender to inevitability.

Everything changes —
craggy eyes, body sags,
dying season extends.
You make me smile.

Standing at the edge of town watching
you descend the PATH stairway,
a come to life Springsteen song.

Obviously.

That was fun

says the singer after the first song.
Glad to see friends I haven't seen
Let's rock
Let's move
Let's sweat together

The next band tortures the sound man
or maybe vice versa as they take the stage
and launch into a pop tune about a heroin overdose.
"The next song's for the ladies — *she's a killer.*"

It's a 95 degree day outside,
still I'm dressed wrong in shorts and tee
like a NJ dad or grandad adrift
in a sea of black jeans, miniskirts, Converse,
and pointy Trash and Vaudeville boots
on a Friday night at Bowery Electric

Grooving to the The Cynz,
dreading the sweltering path ride home.
Cyndi the singer is beautiful,
she thinks I'm cute.
At 64 years old what does that mean?
Honestly, what has it ever meant?

The world is different tonight.
Am I too dim to recognize
the reckoning, the shift,
the churning dynamo of
a world in flux?

One more scotch and soda.
Turn around, look
in the bathroom mirror,
hold in my gut —
I look good
I am alive
We are alive
Rock on!

Lobster Dance

Standing on the Bowery
waiting on a friend
ready for the show
flush with existential dread
searching for a metaphor
to match his falcons' gyre
you wish to write like Yeats
but all you've got is vultures
circling towards the fire.

Instead, you tread the
grimy thick jawed street
a moonlit shadow, unsure,
one more menace on the prowl,
more Esau than Jacob,
three generations
from shtetl removed.
Still, the stars beam your way.

The rock and rollers
of Hoboken soar tonight.
Broken wing, siren song,
Jim Mastro record drop
Bowery Electric
5th scotch and soda
holding onto the rail
as Karyn Kuhl
serenades the room,
guitars beseeching
the lobster dance
flying high above
deep in the night.

You teeter to the subway
screeching underground
wondering how to fit in
and why the locals
never offer you a ride
across the river
back home.

Autumn Sketches (2020)

What the Dog Walkers Said

Hoboken's like a cult
they sit in their cubicles all day
working working working
then they turn into werewolves
Thursday and Friday night

It's crazy they sure like to party

Wonder how they vote?

Late

On my walk today
I noticed a new Halloween superstore
on the site of what had been Modells.
I wanted to go in but as I got closer
I realized today is November 5
and the store is dark.

Power

In this season of discontinence
I have discovered new powers
I can walk as far as my bladder allows
the soccer field
the boat house
the train station
Sinatra Park
the financial center
between two cars
on a deserted
west side street.

Branding

A line in front of CityMD snakes
around the corner
50 feet away a group of maskless men
crowd around a sidewalk tv
as the Jets lose once again
Across the street in front of McDonalds
a homeless man waits
with empty paper cup
in outstretched hand
the Trump motorcade
drives down Washington Street
horns blaring
flags waving.

Joy

I feel joy
though I wish my sister Carol
was alive for the election results,
to see the dancing in the streets
the banging of pots and pans.
Caroline and I stumble through
town drunk on noontime champagne
in this uncanny November sun.

Report from My Son

The bagel line was long
Jesus was out begging for change
Everyone looked hungover
another Hoboken Sunday morning.

III.

Raging Bull

This happened before I was born,
when my sisters Carol and Susan were very young,
the early 50's. Our family lived in a one bedroom
apartment on Sheraton Avenue, behind the Grand
Concourse in the Bronx, right by Yankee Stadium.

One night a child was crying incessantly
followed by adults yelling at each other
at the top of their lungs.
My father opened the window
and yelled down into the courtyard,
"Won't you shut that child up?
What's wrong with you people?
We're trying to sleep around here."

An angry voice yelled up,
"Oh yeah, who the hell are you
to tell us to shut up? Get down here
and we'll settle this like men.
Get down here so I can kick your ass!"

My dad went to the door to get his jacket
ready to rumble. It was at that point
that my mom said to him, "Sounds like that racket
is coming from the LaMotta's downstairs."

For the next half hour a steady stream
of profanities reverberated through the courtyard,
"Get down here so I can kick your ass, you big pussy.
Nobody talks to me like that. Get down here."

My dad took off his jacket, turned out the lights,
closed the window, pulled down the shades
and sat quietly in his chair in the dark
smoking cigarette after cigarette.

Family History (According to Carol)

Carol is my sister.
She is 13 years older than me.
She is suffering from ALS and Dementia.
A few years ago I did the ALS Challenge
and posted it on Facebook.
I got 167 likes.
Now it's real.

"Carol is the smart one," I joke to the new social worker.
"I was a teacher . . ."
"She is well respected in her field," I elaborate.
"The nazis killed our whole family."
"Not really, otherwise we wouldn't be here," I correct.
"They killed our brother."
"That's true," I affirm.

"I'm sorry," says the social worker.

"When I was little, Susan threw my toys out the window
of our 4th floor apartment in the Bronx," says Carol.
"I'm sorry," says the social worker.
"She tried to throw Danny out the window,
but I saved him and put him on the couch."
"That's why I'm here now," I tell the social worker.

"Susan is crazy, is that what's happening to me?"
"Our sister is autistic and schizophrenic and retarded," I chime in.
"You're not supposed to say retarded anymore," Carol corrects.
"I know, but she is."

"No offense taken," says the social worker.

"My husband Rich was abused when he was little."
"That's what he says," I add.
"Danny thinks we should be divorced, but he's a good man."
"No, he's not," I correct.
"Our mother was crazy, I think it runs in the family."
"No Carol, Mom was just fragile."
"Donald Trump is a nazi."

"I won't argue the point," the social worker and I reply
simultaneously.

Carol is doing what Mom used to do,
which always embarrassed me,
she's telling her sad story to a stranger.
Now I'm doing it.

"You're lucky, you have a brother who looks out for you,"
says the social worker.
"The nazis killed our brother. I want a cigarette, can you
light it for me?"
"Of course," I say.
"Dad always said, turn out the lights."

I want to run out of the apartment and scream
and rage between the cars in the parking lot.
I want to tear my flesh and throw rocks
through windows to hear the sound of breaking glass.

I sit at the table and refocus the conversation,
"We need help . . ."

About Forgetting

Perhaps the only way that my sister Carol
in her 76th year can escape the darkness
is to forget the details
of finances and friendships,
to quietly withdraw
from the ugliness engulfing us.

I won't allow her to forget
she's my big sister
and we were put here
to spite the nazis
who still give us nightmares.

Two refugees
who lost everything
came together
so we could be born
in this strange new land,
replacements
for our murdered brother.

I want her to remember
the precocious child
who skipped two grades
because back then
that's how we dealt
with gifted children.

But Carol has already begun
the business of forgetting:
Forgetting the foldout

living room couch
in the one bedroom
Bronx apartment she shared
with our parents
and schizophrenic sister Susan.

Forgetting she practically raised me,
Mom's nervous breakdown
weeks after I was born.

She vaguely remembers marrying
Leo at 20 years old
attempting to provide
a "good Jewish home."
The laughable congratulations
from Leo's parents
for landing a scholar
though our working-class Dad
called him "that lazy bastard."

Carol has not yet forgotten
she was one of this country's
first certified ESL teachers,
well-respected in her field.
The years of her career lost
raising three bright, healthy,
curious children.
"At least I raised interesting children,"
she tells me.
"Not like *his* kids,
those dullards."

She can't seem to forget Roy Cohn,
the family boogieman
long dead, unable
to harm us anymore.

It might hurt to recall
how after 34 years of marriage
she left Leo for Rich, a needy man
sixteen years her junior
because she had grown tired
of being ignored.

Carol can't seem to remember
Rich has stolen
and is still stealing
tens of thousands of her dollars
earned working two jobs
while he sat home without a job —
and now it's my job
to try to get it back.
Her baby brother
today big brother.

She has forgotten
she asked me four times
in the past three days
to give her seven thousand dollars
to pay off Rich's credit card.
And she's forgotten
that the answer remains no.

When the screaming,
the whining, the finger pointing
become unbearable, a retreat

into an imagined past
where steady progress
was the trajectory of life
and evolution a law of nature,
may be the only way out.
This isn't nostalgia;
it's an attempt to fix memory.

Footnote

Carol, today you thanked me 5 times
for taking you to the doctor,
but remember
this is what we do in our family.
It's what Dad did for his sisters,
it's what you did for Mom,
it's what you and I did for Susan,
it's what I do for you.
This is what we do.

Dispossession

The family never speaks of Lena
but here she is, my aunt
from my father's side
in the snack aisle at Acme
that used to be A&P
that used to be Foodtown
that used to be Pathmark
that used to be ShopRite
down the block from us
in Hoboken, NJ.

Lena stands in the snack section
weighing a bag of pretzels
versus a bag of Doritos.
What foodstuffs in this new
land of wonder? I follow her
to the canned goods —
Progresso Soups, Chunky Soups
Campbell's Soups, Well Yes! Soups,
the flavors, the variety,
all unkosher, all available,
all on sale. Buy 3, get 5 free,
what sense does that make?

Jesus stands in front of the liquor
section silent, newly dead.
I saw his body at Our Lady
of Saints. One of the few people
I met who looked better
in the coffin than he did
on the streets. Jesus's name

is Bobby. He was a homeless
man who lived between 6th and 7th
Street on the Avenue, the stretch
between the bagel shop and Dunkin
Donuts his domain. He's holding a Bud
tallboy in a brown paper bag. "Thanks,"
he says, the only word he ever says
besides "smoke?" when he sees me
walking down the street. I nod to him
in my usual way and follow Lena
to the meat section, far from the pork
chops to the cuts of beef. So many
choices, what's a lonely apparition to do?
She surveys the possibilities
sometimes picks up a package
for inspection, moving her lips
as she reads the label.

Lena was killed at Auschwitz.
But we don't talk about that.
Her father, my grandfather
drove her out of the house
with a raised garden hoe
after her pregnancy became
apparent. She moved across
Frankfurt with her boyfriend
the army sergeant who disappeared
somewhere along the line.
Her blonde-haired children
Wanda and Denny murdered
at Theresienstadt. Family history
we don't talk about. I don't
talk about. I'm the only one left.

Today Lena is shopping at Acme
and Jesus is eyeing her as she touches
the plums, so delicious, so out of season
on this gray autumn day. He follows her
as she glides down the produce aisle
past the scales and cabbages and spinach
and lettuce and brussels sprouts
until she gets to the front of the store
and sees the pumpkins. What are these
orange monstrosities? Only in America.
If only America.

Jesus takes her by the hand
past the sad cashiers into the parking lot
where the shopping carts are scattered
willy-nilly like the souls of her brothers
and sisters. They walk off the supermarket
grounds and disappear into
what's left of this day,
what's left of this world.

Hawk from a Handsaw

My father was often at a loss for words . . .
His name — Siegfried a source of confusion;
half his friends called him Ziggy, the other half Fred.
He wasn't worse at English than your average immigrant
but he didn't speak as good as my mom whose English
wasn't so great, but still she made fun of his accent.
Da dinx was his all-purpose catch phrase
which I realized years after his death meant "the things"
when Issa, my Senegalese friend said the same thing.
Bibbis was penis, *popo* the butt,
da volks were the neighbors, *landsman* meant Jew.
Music was his passion with Sunday's reserved
for the record player as he conducted the symphonies
of Mahler and Schuman as sister Susan swayed spastically
to the lilting melodies of the great composers
while I sat on the couch sucking my thumb.

My mom was more loquacious
often putting inspirational quotes —
President Kennedy, Spinoza, and Bertrand Russell
over the kitchen sink in an attempt to make her life
as a housewife in suburban NJ bearable.
When no one was around she spoke to the radio.

Susan, institutionalized since I was born
has a vocabulary of maybe 20 words:
pot roast, rainbow cookies, cheese, 'nilla pudding,
go back, Danny Boy, Mommy's coming?

I'll never know brother Ernst's last words
probably spoken between the train and the gas
though I know it was German, I hope it was merciful,
if mercy is a word we can use.

Carol was an English teacher, the first high school
graduate in our family. The smart one.
She lost her ability to speak, or read the *New Yorker*
in her final year of life. In the end, what was left to say?

The prodigal son, I fancy myself a poet.
Probably I'm delusional,
barely audible outside a small circle of friends
words, words, words . . .
I can't stop

Luck

Let's raise a glass to Yiddle Giddle Dovid
the hunchback of Kolmar, Poland.
A distant relative of my grandfather Solly
as was most everyone in the shtetl.
May his memory be a blessing!

The boys would rub his hump for luck
on the way to shul. The village was divided
as to whether Yiddle was an idiot
or a holy fool: "A single coin in an empty jar
makes the most noise." Yiddle met his demise
falling into the community cesspool.

It's been said that he could have been saved,
but none of the townspeople were brave enough
to go in after him. Much to my family's shame.

When Caroline goes on a genealogy bender
and tells our sons they are related
to George Washington and James Monroe
and various founders of our nation,
I remind them Yiddle Giddle Dovid
lurks in their not-so-distant past
begging change in another world:
"With money in my pocket I am wise,
handsome and I sing well too."

Doris

All I wanted was to never lose him.
Whenever we went out to a nightclub
or a sidewalk café, women would come
over and make remarks about how handsome he was.
We got married in 1937 and I
was the happiest bride in the world.

My brother Hans had his Bar Mitzvah in 1937.
At the party I was introduced to a very handsome
young man, any young girl's dream.
He was tall and slender with bright blue eyes,
a straight nose, a pink complexion, dark hair.
On top of this he was a good dresser.
I was 17 and madly in love.

His name was Ludwig Lesser
and he was quite the charmer.
We dated, we danced at the Moka Efti,
he bought me flowers,
I visited him in his room, and we made love.

The romance was beautiful,
the marriage, not so great.
First off, I was pregnant,
and I had morning sickness,
which lasted for five months.
I was nauseous all the time.

Ludwig and I moved into a small apartment
in Berlin N.W. My father had to pay our rent.
My husband left me alone for weeks,

going on a tour selling Oriental carpets.
He didn't send any money.
I was pregnant, alone, and without food,
too embarrassed and proud to go back to my parents.

Our furniture was taken away
because he did not pay support
for his other two children.
Yes, he had two girlfriends
and each one had a child by him.
Yet I still loved him.

We were married for 8 months.
The divorce was September 7, 1937.
The divorce left a wound
and I never trusted men again.
The ones I pick are often the gangster
type or the straying type
or the selfish type but not
the decent type of man.
Who knows, maybe men are just that way.

Ludwig had a very persuasive lawyer
and I had one who stuttered.
I was left with nothing,
just a couple of Oriental carpets
and a soon to be born son.

My son Ernst was born
six days later on 13 September.
My beautiful little boy,
only four and a half pounds
but he gained weight very quickly.

I nursed him a whole year,
and I had milk enough
for more children.

2.

13 June, 1946

Dear Sir,

I ask your help on getting information on the following matter.
While reading the German-Jewish newspaper the *Aufbau*
I saw a list with names of Jewish children who were saved.
In August 1939 I left my little son Ernst Lesser
born 13 September 1937 with my parents in Berlin.
In 1943 my mother, father, and boy were sent East,
I don't know where. I haven't heard from my people again.
Do you maybe have his name on your list?
Is there any way to find out if my child is alive?
He would be nine years old now.
Please let me know if you can find my boy.
I appreciate your help and maybe some answers.
My brother Johnny, who was an interpreter
for General Patton says everything is lost.
My American husband says I need to move on.
Thank you for your help.

— Doris

3.

My parents always emphasized
that we were German Jewish
and our family had deep roots in Germany.
We weren't even that.

Our ancestors came from Poland
and Galicia by Ukraine.
My parents only a generation removed
from the shtetl. The one who objected
to this hypocrisy was my grandmother
Leah who thought the posturing ridiculous.
She was an orthodox woman
whose faith in God never faltered,
maybe not even after she was deported
to Theresienstadt. I wouldn't know.

When I was forced to attend Christian religious lessons,
my grandmother came to our apartment and protested.
No Jewish granddaughter or grandson of hers,
daughter of a Rabbi from Lvov which the Germans
call Lemberg and everyone pronounces differently.
The Christian lessons were discontinued
for Hans and me. I will be forever grateful.
Other than my father and Hans and me,
nobody liked her. Everybody else thought
she was an old, bitter, bitchy woman.

In 1935 my parents decided to take me out of school.
Boarding school was their decision.
I spent my whole 15th year in Lausanne
learning French and getting fat on chocolates.
During evenings, the sun turned
the mountain peaks into white and golden domes.
I was homesick. I missed the hustle
and bustle of Berlin.
The school year over, I went home to my family.
To hell with the mountains.

4.

My parents bought me a camera for my 18th birthday.
That's why there's so many photographs,
my father loved taking pictures.
I barely got to touch it.
Here's one of Ernst and me at the Tiergarten,
the zoo, we lived right near it.
He'd just learned to walk which is why
it looks like he's on a leash.
In this one, he's wearing a little outfit
it must be for a party, maybe his 4th birthday?
They sent me pictures every month.
Until they stopped.

The Golden Path

— From Moses to Moses there's no one like Moses

You got time on your hands . . .
You go to the Maimonides exhibit
at the Center of Jewish History.
You go because it's your nephew's middle name,
a little bit that, and some genuine curiosity.

Illuminated manuscripts, philosophical treatises,
medical journals, portraits, basketball jerseys,
the whole megillah . . . The Golden Path,
Rambam, Moses ben Maimon,
Guide for the Perplexed,
you're lost in your Jewishness.

You wander upstairs.
On the second floor you stumble
into an exhibit titled EXILE.
You look at a display for Florence Mendheim.
You say to yourself, *she has the same name*
as Mom's maiden name.
Reading her bio you think
how strange, Mom's cousin Florie
was a NYC librarian just like Florence.
You read on: Florence Mendheim was a spy
against the nazis and a hero.
Pretending to be a nazi sympathizer
and working under various aliases,
she'd gather names, take notes and collect
pro-nazi and anti-Semitic material
in various New York neighborhoods
for the American Jewish Congress.

Then it dawns on you.
You go down to the main desk
and tell a man working the counter
that you think a person who has an exhibit
devoted to them is your cousin, or second cousin.
He doesn't give a shit.
So, you go back to the second floor
and hover over a man and a woman
who seem to be talking business.
After about 5 minutes the man asks, "Can I help you?"
You explain that you're cousins,
pointing to a photo of Florie.
His eyes light up.
He's the curator.
He says she's a really big deal around here,
which is why her display is next to Albert Einstein's.
He takes your picture next to the photo.
You feel bad that you're dressed bummy
in shorts and a tee shirt.
He says they'd been looking for living relatives
of Florence Mendheim for over a decade.
Here you are. Here we are.

Relativity

His mouth is open. This is what happens in death. No need for metaphor. I'd like to say he looks at peace, but at peace is a phrase none of us would use to describe Leo. The oxygen tube is still connected. I pull Jean, wife number 3 from the body. But she won't let go.

Leo is my brother-in-law, and after he and my sister Carol divorced 20 years ago, he is still my brother-in-law because that's how it is in our family. Time is relative.

A week ago, he tells me that the new Marilyn Monroe movie is disturbing because modern movies no longer take into account the existence of God.

A nurse comes into the room. Raab his youngest son stands over the bed. Jessica his oldest texts those who should know. Jean is crying, the nurse is indifferent, I want to make everything right.

Leo sets out to prove that the concepts of Chance and God are interchangeable, always looking for a unified theory, a la Einstein, of everything.

Leo is in constant battle with his children Jessica, David, and Raab, 3rd wife Jean, 2nd wife Sue, 1st wife Carol, various drugstore clerks, medical professionals, and students in his Applied Mathematics and Statistics classes at NYC Technical College who fail to live up to a revolving set of expectations.

"Every successful story begins with a lie," he tells me. "Tell me a lie, something along the lines of I have a massive cock, or I am a virtuous man," he suggests, "and then you'll have a

story. You're a writer, I want to read your story before I die."
"But I am a virtuous man," I protest weakly.

A man of obsessions: Coca-Cola, Jewish deli food, electronic gizmos, theories of probability, and the writings of Yuval Noah Harari which he tries to fit into a cohesive theory of history and the future of humanity, precipitating a 5-year argument that I am ill equipped to win.

"Did you read the poem by Dante?" he asks. "*Purgatorio*? That's my life now, hooked up to machines undergoing dialysis 3 times a week in this drab basement with the other poor souls awaiting final judgment."

I'm allowed to smoke when people die. It's a rule I made up. No guilt whatsoever. Leo would approve.

"Cursing is a form of prayer," he tells us. "Jean doesn't believe me. She thinks I'm just an angry old man. They don't like cursing in the Philippines. They believe God is watching them. Silly."

For his 75th birthday I buy tickets for us to see Harari speak at the 92nd Street Y. I slink down in my seat as Leo shouts from the audience at the Israeli interviewer, "Let him speak! it's not about you. You people have no fucking manners."

I am the witness to Leo's marriage to Sue, wife number 2. Sue is locked in a Chinese mental institution. She leaves Leo to go back home to visit family. While there she stays at a 5-star hotel in Beijing racking up enormous charges saying she is the wife of a wealthy American industrialist. After a month, government officials take her away. The marriage is annulled by joint agreement between the Chinese government and the U.S. State Department.

Leo does my taxes, an event unto itself. Me sitting over his shoulder making up numbers with him cursing and gesticulating as he makes up even bigger numbers. This goes on for over 30 years. Now I go to an accountant and every year I pay a lot of money to the taxman. When Leo did my taxes, Uncle Sam paid me.

After Carol leaves, I take him to the Frontier Room for a beer to help settle his rattled nerves. After two beers he asks "How many of these are we going to drink? Have you ever thought you might have a drinking problem?" This from the man who regularly drinks 6 bottles of Coke a day.

"Do you like men?" he asks.
"Huh?" What do you mean?"
"You call yourself a poet."
"I don't call myself anything."
"Ginsberg likes men."
"True."
"Does he like you?"
"Not enough," I admit.
"Just don't drag your friend Katz into this. He's capable of great things."

Leo calls the Dean's office after my photo appears over the cash register at the Rutgers Bookstore with the caption "Do not cash checks from this man," after a third bounced check from an account I share with my mom who cannot manage our finances. From then on, Leo is my financial advisor.

I call it Timespace. Sometimes Spacetime. The idea that the two are codependent. Events happen in a place, but also a time. The time and place bond us. We are time travelers, we have gotten from our birth to this very moment right now. I tell this to Leo. He laughs, "That's basic Physics 101. Everybody knows that." I light a cigarette.

Memory flash: First day of college. Me saying goodbye, my mother grasping onto the door frame as Leo pulls her legs as my new roommates watch in amazement.

Leo takes me to a drug den in Washington Heights run by his students, piles of marijuana on a large kitchen table and smaller mounds of white powder on a side table, a big safe, old fashioned adding machine on top. Driving over the bridge he asks, "So what have you learned today?" "Well," I answer, "in order to be successful, you have to be willing to take chances, but only after doing a risk reward analysis." "Exactly," he says, "those guys have what it takes, they're hungry. Remember that."

Lenrow's Drugstore. Sixteen-year-old me follows him to the counter. "I'd like a 12 pack of condoms for my brother-in-law, regular size will do. He says he's having sex, I'm not sure I believe him, but I don't want him knocking up any Dumont girls before he's off to college." I want to run, but Leo holds on to my sleeve.

Leo steps up after dad passes away. Carol is the encouraging one, Leo is the one with high expectations, occasionally unrealistic ones regarding me. It's Leo who decides I will study pre-medicine "because the family needs a doctor." I go along and the results are predictable.

I am the unwitting foil to numerous get-rich-quick schemes, especially after my father passes away. Leo constantly finds paying work for me: the car wash in Westwood where us 15 year-olds are treated like orphans in a Dickens novel.

Mr. Thompson the elderly electrician whom Leo convinces to take me on as an apprentice, a job that ends after 2 weeks when I almost electrocute him. There's the brilliant plan of selling folding fishing chairs to poor souls waiting on line in Hackensack to file their unemployment claims during the recession of 1973. That scheme falls apart after the police detain me for questioning and Leo drives off to fend for myself.

Leo is a historically bad driver. Not soon after my father dies Leo takes it upon himself to teach my mother to drive. After about 15 minutes of showing Mom the basics, Leo says, "Okay Doris, you follow me. Do just like I showed you." Within two minutes my mom has totaled the car meant for me by driving head on into a telephone pole on Bedford Avenue.

I am his copilot on forays into the Lower East Side to get pickles on Essex Street or new underground comic books in Greenwich Village. Often, I wait in the double-parked car, "If the police come, just drive around the block," he advises. "But Leo, I'm 13 years old!"

Screaming matches at the Passover seder, sometimes in Yiddish, sometimes English between Leo and his mother Bronia, his mother and his father Paul, and sometimes cousin Moishe and his mother. The insults hurled across the table are legendary, "I should have had an abortion like your father wanted."

My father chides Carol, the apple of his eye, about Leo's driving: "You're supposed to be a teacher. You say you taught him how to drive. What kind of teacher are you?"

In our backyard on Forest Road my dad, the 5 foot 4 fitness buff after perhaps one too many beers challenges Leo to a wrestling match. My father aggressively wraps his arms around Leo's lower half and tries to take him down before Leo gently picks him up with both arms and throws him across the yard.

My father gets dentures. To accomplish this, his remaining teeth are pulled. I refuse to stay in the house with toothless dad, so I am sent to Ithaca where Leo and Carol live while he finishes grad school at Cornell. They have cool friends; my mom calls them beatniks. After two weeks of missing school, my parents retrieve me. I hold onto Leo as if my life depends on it.

Black and white photo. Carol and Leo's wedding, June 1964. Me in my little red jacket (I remember), the baby of the family. First Dad, then Mom, then Carol, now Leo. Everyone's gone. Of course. I still travel through time.

The glee on Leo's face when my mother laughs at Bronia, after she says how lucky we are to get a scholar in our family. In my parents' eyes, Carol, the first person in our family to go to college, actually the first person to graduate high school, is the scholar of our clan.

1942, Vilna. Buried in straw covered pit to hide from nazis. For two years Paul, Bronia, and Leo travel east by oxcart through the Soviet Union all the way to Japan. Another year west to Berlin by the end of the war. Displaced Persons Camp. Loss. Lost. The Bronx. America.

Gravity. The speed of light. Time. History. Chance. Relativity. Frame of reference. Probability. Survival. Cigarette smoke curling upwards to God or nothing. Rise.

These Days (2020)

We said our goodbyes and told stories about Bob
my father-in-law at the cemetery in August.
We told our stories and said goodbye to my sister Carol
at the funeral home in July.
We drank wine and watched scary movies at Mary Anne's
in June in an attempt to forget the world.
We drove north and west and hiked in unknown parks in May.
We went for long walks in April and pissed on deserted streets.
We sheltered in place, watched cable news and tried to stay
out of each other's way in March.

I am frightened by my family's fear
as well as the lack of fear by strangers.
Most everyone has become a stranger,
the smiles behind the masks unseen.
I religiously plod today's 10,000 steps.
The USA dismantled by design
as we bounce between crises.

There will be live music again and dancing
and the remnants of a social life.
We have said our goodbyes.
Let's meet again further on
down this mislaid jigsaw boulevard.

IV.

Languish (or 3 moods in 3 hours)

1.

Sometimes you don't want to go out.
What's there to do, really?
There are only two roads out of town.
Your feet know them by heart.
You've visited the stores on the Avenue
repeatedly and worry the help will think
you have no life, which is true but you prefer
they not come to that conclusion yet.
Your car is tired of driving to the same places:
the supermarket, Home Depot, your sister's group home.
The dogs on the street don't acknowledge your existence
the geese and goslings are not scared of you
and neither is that gang of boys riding
chopped bikes past without regard.
Almost all relationships have become long distance
affairs, and we know what happens to them.
You gaze at everyone and everything
and are somewhat amazed.

2.

Funerals are not that important.
You've curated your funeral the past 30 years
down to the set list, the guest list
and who gets to read a poem.
What's important is the sense of loss
felt by those you've left behind.
Your romantic heart beating:
what-if's, should'ves and why-nots.
You have finally come to understand

nobody's as happy as they are on Facebook
nobody's as angry as they are on Twitter
nobody's as beautiful as they are on Instagram
everyone's as desperate as they seem . . .

3.

You don't ask for much —
a walk through Central Park on a sunny day
a bottle of wine with friends at an outdoor cafe
Jacob deGrom blazing heat against the Braves
orchestra seats for a new Tom Stoppard play
new pathways of thought as you turn gray
fresh declarations of love graffitied on the Palisades
this God Damn imposter syndrome to fade away.
Recognizing the bewildered smile on a lost friend's face.

How to Look Good at 60

you don't.

but . . .
you can try.

give up the notion
of black hair.
you'll look like Gary Glitter
who, as we all know
sits in a Vietnamese prison
for soliciting child prostitutes.

facial hair is a plus
it hides the sunken chin
and neck wattle.
if you're a woman,
may the force be with you.

listen to your favorite music
whatever style
move to the beats
no matter how awkward
or white you feel.

write poems as you walk
flow to the rhythm of your feet
or perfect that million-dollar idea
you've been keeping from the world.

change your preferred libations seasonally.
don't let your favored drink get old.

frequent different happy hour spots
and never fear the nightcap.

visit neighborhoods you haven't
set foot in for years. guess what?
they change.

even if your hearing or sight
isn't what it once was
listen with fresh ears
see with open eyes.
believe me, you haven't
seen it all.
most importantly, don't
forget to breathe
breathe in
breathe out
breathe in
breathe out . . .
there,
lookin' good.

Legacy

I offer advice when asked,
usually something along the lines
of "you'll figure it out."
Both my sons are teachers
Casey teaches science, Levi history.
I must have made it look easy (though it wasn't):
those summers watching baseball
and *Sons of Anarchy* on the couch.
When they were in grade school
teachers used to ask, "How do you do it?"
as if we had some magical parenting wisdom
when in fact we had two well-behaved
boys who were simply born that way.

Each boy, though I should call them men,
has a partner named Meghan, whom I adore.
Each Meghan with a family not ours,
that my boys navigate with aplomb
(though I wonder why we don't hang out more).
Hopefully it's not fear of embarrassment.
The Meghans . . . who'd have predicted?

I enjoy spending time with my sons, which I guess
keeps me young while making me feel old.
Each is quiet, you might call them shy,
a defense mechanism perhaps developed growing
up in the home of a needy minor poet.

They live in a different world than the one which I was raised.
Both born and bred Hobokenites, products of public schools
our white friends seek to avoid, while Caroline and I

still newcomers in the city we've lived for 35 years.
Neither much of a Jew, but neither Christian either, thank God.
Raised with few rules, both have strong moral codes
which I imagine they inherited from Caroline,
with Mayflower roots and Episcopal sense of justice.

I want a grandchild or four but as Caroline reminds
it doesn't matter what I want, though I want,
while young enough to leave a trace of memory.
I worry about future life for my sons and their families
unlike my parents who could never escape their past.

Today I tell the same story for the 3rd or 4th time
and see Levi raise his eyebrows to Meghan
who raises her eyebrows to the other Meghan.
I smile to myself content that all is as it should be.
I wish them well, they have the foundation,
two good men in a cockeyed world.

Clothes (Make the Man)

Hoboken waterfront
in your new tee shirt:
Secret Jewish Space Laser Corps
a few knowing smiles,
quizzical looks —
proud in the confines of your city,
reluctant in less forgiving environs.

Old photos show an immigrant boy
dressed by his parents
in the fashion of 1930s Berlin:
schoolboy cap, black blazer
and slacks, colored vest
matching bowtie and pocket square posing
in front of a 1956 Chevy Belair
on the grounds
of Rockland Psychiatric Hospital,
the Sunday sojourn
to sister Susan, institutionalized
weeks after your birth.

Clothes of your past lives:
fashion faux pas
the choices that hit it right.
The blue striped bell bottoms
sister Carol bought you in 8th grade
after years of thrift store
baggy pants with elastic waist
your mom gave you
as school wear throughout
the psychedelic ‘60s.

Self-styled 8th grade revolutionary
you fought to change the dress code
so girls could wear pantsuits to class
and after school activities.

Your mother bought you
pastel-colored briefs
in the Sears bargain basement
creating a stir
in the locker room
gym class a mix
of grades including
19 and 20-year-olds
still in high school
to evade the Vietnam draft.

You saved up your money
for a checkered red and white
Italian restaurant shirt
with black satin shoulders
bought at the local head shop —
so proud of that one,
until you overheard
your boss at the pizza parlor
tell a coworker, "Oh no,
he's wearing that Bozo shirt again."

The navy bell bottoms
you bought used
at the Army Navy
store even though
they were heavy
wool and hot
as hell and

most inconvenient
when you had to pee,
having to open a panel
of twelve mutinous buttons
before relief.

The many flannel shirts
inherited
from your father at 15
when he died.
Invariably two sizes
too large but fitting
your Neil Young
wannabe junkie
early '70s aesthetic.

Somewhere between New
Brunswick and Princeton
for 5 dollars each
at Consalata Mission
thrift store you and your
girlfriend bought a pair
of suede jackets —
the *it* couple of Rutgers University
(in your mind).

The gratitude you felt
when your china
department coworker
suggested two or three
high quality cotton shirts
frequently washed
are a better investment
than ten cheap polyesters

that have a tendency to stink
in the sultry
8th floor air
of Macy's Herald Square.

The purple skin-tight satin pants
taken from your roommate's closet
one hungover Tuesday morning
before going in to teach
a rambunctious Brooklyn
special ed class
causing a commotion
you were unable to contain.

Your teacher wardrobe
sits useless
in your overstocked
closet: collared white shirts,
blue shirts, striped shirts,
checked shirts that you hope
to never have to tuck in
to sensible chino
or corduroy slacks
ever again.

The joy on Bill's face,
your father-in-law's roommate
though a good five years younger
than you, wasting away
in the nursing home, when you
gave him that Ramones tee shirt
with pink lettering
that made you look
like an aging punk sausage

but made him look
like the real deal
before he disappeared
from your life forever.

For no reason at all
you try on
the custom-tailored
blue suit
you just spent
a small fortune on
for the wedding
of your son's friend.
You know you look good
though the photos give
the impression of a mafia boss.
You sometimes fret
what occasion will grant
the opportunity to wear it
again before the day
of your own funeral arrives.

Note Written (by me) on a FB Post of a Friend

Anti-Semitism is
anti-Semitism is
anti-Semitism.
It can't be censored out
nor covered up
nor explained away
by moral equivocators
of the right or the left.

Most gentiles don't get it
though we sure do
and know it when we see it.
Not all anti-Zionists
are anti-Semitic,
we understand that.
But a hell of lot of them are,
we understand that too.

Anti-Semitism is
the President of the United States
equating torch bearing nazis
with anti-fascist counter protestors,
being nicknamed Ike the Kike
by your high school drinking buddies
and going along with it,
being ashamed of your refugee parents
for their foreign ways,
being ashamed.

Anti-Semitism is
the murder of Jews in the Pittsburgh synagogue,
the swastika scrawl in the professor's office,

Alice Walker promoting a holocaust
denier as a purveyor of truth,
Kanye going death con 3.

Anti-Semitism is
the failure to speak up.

Eight Days of Hanukkah (2019)

(a found poem)

Hanukkah came early this year — a shooting
that killed 5 in a Jersey City kosher market
blocks away from the school where my son teaches.

On the first day of Hanukkah a 65-year-old man was punched
and kicked in Manhattan by another man yelling, "Fuck you, Jew!"

On the same day, a group of teenagers attacked a 6-year-old boy
and a 7-year-old boy, striking them from behind.

On the second day of Hanukkah a group of people began yelling anti-Semitic slurs at a 25-year old man as he walked. One of them threw their drink at him.

Also in Brookyln, a 56-year-old man said a group of people
approached him and one of them punched him.

On Christmas Day, a 40-year-old man dressed in "traditional religious clothing" was approached by an individual who blocked his path. That individual punched the victim in the face when the man tried to let him pass.

On the fifth day of Hanukkah a woman was charged with assault as a hate crime after she allegedly attacked a 34-year-old Jewish woman in front of her 3-year-old child.

On the sixth day of Hanukkah Tiffany Harris, 30, was arrested and charged with harassment as a hate crime after she slapped three women in the face while yelling anti-Semitic slurs.

Also on that day a man walked into the Chabad World Headquarters and threatened to shoot and kill people in the center.

On the seventh day of Hanukkah five people were injured when a man walked into a party in a rabbi's home in the suburb of Monsey and stabbed them with a machete.

A Hanukkah miracle on the eighth day — no reported hate crimes in New York. And we beheld the lull in violence as proof of God's love.

Heinrich Heine Reconsiders

1.

I can't decide if it's easy or difficult to pass judgment, so I won't. According to family lore we are the offspring of Heinrich Heine. There are black and white photos of my sisters and me posing at the Lorelei Fountain at Joyce Kilmer Park in the Bronx near where I was born which prove absolutely nothing.

The story goes like this, Heinrich was madly in love with his cousin, a relationship frowned upon by the family who put an unceremonious end to it. Heinrich, the enfant terrible then fell in love with her sister, also his cousin, with whom he fathered a child.

The baby was put up for adoption and this child grew to become my great great grandmother who gave birth to Leah Weishaus (great grandmother), who was murdered at Theresienstadt along with her daughter Feodora (grandmother), who was murdered at Auschwitz along with her husband Solly Mendheim (grandfather) and grandson, Ernst Lesser, my brother, in 1943.

2. The Poet Speaks

My bastards will thank me
To not bear the weight of my name.

Much good the counterfeit conversion
to my grandchildren at Auschwitz.

Wherever books are burned, they will
also in the end burn human beings.

Can my descendants prove my blood beyond rumor?
If they should care in the lands they're scattered.

I was never a good Jew, more so the Seder's wicked
son questioning the rituals by which we're bound.

The old laws of the tribe not my passion.
God will forgive me, it's his job.

Ring around the smokestacks
Pocketful of gold teeth

Ashes, ashes,
We all disappear.

Slumber

1.

Caroline shakes me awake
"What were you dreaming?"

"Chupacabra," I say, "I was fighting little
chupacabras for a place to suckle

at our mother's many teats."
"Draw it," she says, "make me a picture."

2.

"What the fuck," Caroline says
After I punch her.

"I dreamed you were trying to steal
my breath away. I had to get it back

or die trying," I say before falling
asleep five seconds later.

3.

I stand on stage not remembering
the words or how to play the guitar

useless in my hands. Barefoot
and my feet are bleeding. "This century

has been cruel and unusual," I sputter
to a hearty chorus of boos and derision.

4.

Judging the Comic-Con pageant I caution
the contestants to maintain their distance.

"Look at the knockers on her," says my pal
Mark. "Shhh," I say, "they can hear you."

Upon awaking I wash my hands,
start the coffee, put on my mask

and retrieve the scattered trash
the garbage men have left behind.

Day 228

You've always been impressionable
If you had a dog, you'd write dog poems
Nothing much is happening
Tuesday the same as Monday
which is the same as last Friday
You watch plenty of cable news
but nobody wants to hear about that
You've stopped observing your surroundings
they're the same every day
You've resolved to speak less as you grow older
(in direct opposition to writing more)
out of fear of repeating yourself
like your close friends who you don't know
when you'll see again.

You want to write of joy but fear jinxing
the next 8 days with hopeful speculation
There's always Borat, Tenacious D
and fading memories of times before this all began:
Joining the conga line behind Ruby Dee
as you snake your way through Amiri's
Newark home in celebration of his birthday
Caroline stepping out of the shower naked
at a time you were unconcerned and unashamed
about how your bodies looked
Choking back cigar smoke you and Rob
pretend to enjoy outside St Mary's Hospital
at the birth of your first child
Your students singing Stevie Wonder's "Happy Birthday"
to you on the second day of a new school year
The Hoboken Artists' Studio Tour
Your sister's smile.

Noel

I want you
to love me
for the bastard
I am.
40 years ago
I thought there
would be many
women. Now I know
better. Thank you
for filling the void
admirably. See you
later when my train
arrives. Tim said,
"one more drink,"
I said, "okay"
3 drinks ago.
Not much of a love
poem I know,
but yesterday I carried
the Christmas tree and
haggled its price before
collapsing on the couch
to watch you hang
baubles from branches
exultant in your glory.

Flower

Afraid to lose you
to boredom
another man
another interest
a limey fuckhead
New York City
a renegade cult . . .

And I did —
the dirty glamor
of heroin.

I got the call
at Macy's,
our friend Rob:
"I got some
bad news."

Twenty minutes later
the white flower
interview (Macy's
jargon for manager).
My responses:
"I'm a smart guy . . .
I get along
with other people . . .
I want to make money."
Two months later
done at Macy's.

Yesterday an article
about Basquiat.
Your new boyfriend
who shall remain
unnamed (my prerogative)
was named
his chief
supplier of dope.

At your funeral
the boyfriend took
center stage
weeping, carrying on
like the little
bitch he was
while I stood
on the sidelines
a rock,
how I thought
a man should act
a stoic fuckin rock.

Forty years later
I stand
at your grave
in Titusville
single rose
like Joe DiMaggio.
Red bloom
blue sky
green lawn
earth scratch
scar root.

I don't blame
Lonnie (oops)
for my inability
to hold onto
what could not
be contained —
fear misplaced
the swirl
of time
a life
a place.

CODA

HOPE

(an open letter to posterity from
a minor poet of the 21st century)

Moondog said it long ago . . . Bye bye bye Manhattan
So long Steve Dalachinsky and Steve Cannon
the Grassroots Tavern and Carnegie Deli
St. Mark's Books and Sidewalk Café.
Say adios to living in a zip that starts with 1.
Can we hope again to afford a Yankees game,
a Broadway play or a taxi ride across town?
Where have all the people gone?

This is for you Larry Kelly fighting, fighting, fighting
for breath on the whirring ventilator of fate.
What can we say about hope when there isn't hope?
We can say: It's time to get to work, to clean up the mess
we have left our children and our children's children
as well as our parents' generation so we are seen
in a kinder light by history and any god
who takes an interest in the daily lives of human-kind.

We must retrain ourselves to look for the good
in fellow humans not just mistakes and moments
of weakness. We need to remind ourselves the
measure of life is the journey undertaken
not the rewards we accrue at any given time.
We as a species can still achieve wonders
when pushed and we are pushed in ways
not seen in generations. We need compassion
and community action while living in isolation
and distance by necessity and choice. The screens
we're addicted to offer little solace to the lonely

mortals we've become in spite of our strength
as social creatures who once upon a time
enjoyed each other's company. Time passes
like clouds through a sleepless night haunted
by fever dreams of those we've left behind.

The sirens passing by the front of our house
as common as the chirping of the birds in back.
The morning news infuriates because we know
our president is ill equipped to deal with a crisis
that wouldn't be as bad if he wasn't around.

Let us acknowledge the quiet voices
as well as those who command our ears.
Our shared language is a beautiful creation
not to be sullied by political doublespeak,
the overuse of adverbs, or the ever-evolving
jargon of hate. Let us celebrate the skilled
and unskilled workers who save our lives,
by restoring unions that protect workers
to their rightful place in American society.

Everyone I know is in the process of losing
someone dear to them. I wake up every few hours
with my chest beating wondering who's next?
Every cough is not the end, every breath precious.
A walk outside the house should not be occasion
for an argument with Caroline who I hit last night
in the middle of sleep because I dreamed she was trying
to steal my breath away. I've caught up on reading back copies
of the *New Yorker* and know as much about Bolivian politics
and Fiona Apple's mental state as I'll ever need to know.

My neighbor, a kindly woman, is shouting at passersby
"Wear a mask, don't be an asshole."
I have phoned my teacher friends and empathized
with the conundrum of online teaching while schooling
one's own children home from school. We have come
to learn that quarantine is not a romantic proposition.
There's a time for metaphor and a time for reality
and this shit is real in a way we've rarely seen.

The opposite of hope is despair with fear as a catalyst
favored by demagogues and their shady minions.
Our survival is unsustainable if we dread each other
though right now we must protect ourselves from each
other by distance and social responsibility.

Facebook nostalgia may serve as balm
but hope is the only cure
because without hope none of this matters
without hope none of this mattered.

Thanks

Jack Wiler once said I was lost:
He wrote it in a poem.
I don't think I'm lost.
Lately everyone is so confident
confident they are right
confident they know the way
confident they'll get laid
so sure of how to punish
guilty people on tv.
Often I have nothing in my head.

I'll be walking down the street thinking
I should be thinking about something
but I'm not.
Sometimes I think about where
I parked my car
or if I need a haircut
or why old people don't like loud
music when they're a little deaf
or how I should call my sister
even though she's dead.

Or how the multiplicity of the multiverse
already exists in the form of
8 billion living worlds
each a universe unto itself.
But then I look up at the tree,
its orange autumnal splendor
on the side of Our Lady of Grace
beneath the bluest burst of sky

Hoboken has to offer
and think this is life,
my life, one of billions.
Not too bad at all.
Thank you for this gift.

ACKNOWLEDGMENTS

Some of these poems, at times in different forms, have appeared in the following publications: *Anti Heroin Chic*; *Arbella*; *A Gathering of the Tribes*; *Jew Belong*; *The Nu Review*; *Pine Hills Review*; *Red Fez*; *The Red Wheelbarrow*; *Scribbler*; *Shō*; *209* (Peppertree Press); *Beacon Radiant* (Great Weather for Media); *Life in Quarantine* (Stanford University); *NYC From the Inside* (Blue Light Press)

Thank You:

Eva H.D., Kerry Trautman, Chavisa Woods, Timothy Ree, Teresa Carson, Mara Torres Gonzalez, Debra Fried, Dimitri Reyes, Gabriel Cleveland, Joan Cusack Handler, Baron Wormser, Karyn Kuhl, Roxanne Hoffman, Eliot Katz, Robert Press, reg e gaines, Kevin Powell, Andy Clausen, Raymond Foye, Lisa Creech Bledsoe, Donna Dallas, Jordan Trethewey, Doc Sigerson, Laura Church, Vera Sirota, Bob Foster, Rand Hoppe, Jean-Paul Picard, John Istel, Issa Sow, Carol and Leo Chosid, Caroline, Casey, Levi, Meghan, and Meghan

CavanKerry's Mission

A not-for-profit literary press serving art and community, CavanKerry is committed to expanding the reach of poetry and other fine literature to a general readership by publishing works that explore the emotional and psychological landscapes of everyday life, and to bringing that art to the underserved where they live, work, and receive services.

Other Books in the Florenz Eisman Memorial Series

Dead Things and Where to Put Them, Marina Carreira
The Curve of Things, Kathy Kremins
Tanto Tanto, Marina Carreira
Wonderama, Catherine Doty
WORKS, Danny Shot
Abloom & Awry, Tina Kelley

This book was printed on paper from responsible sources.

The Jersey Slide is typeset in Altivo, a workhorse sans serif created by Serbian designers, Zoran and Nikola Kostić of the Kostić Type Foundry.